SIMPLE AND STYLISH

Weddings

SIMPLE AND STYLISH
Weddings

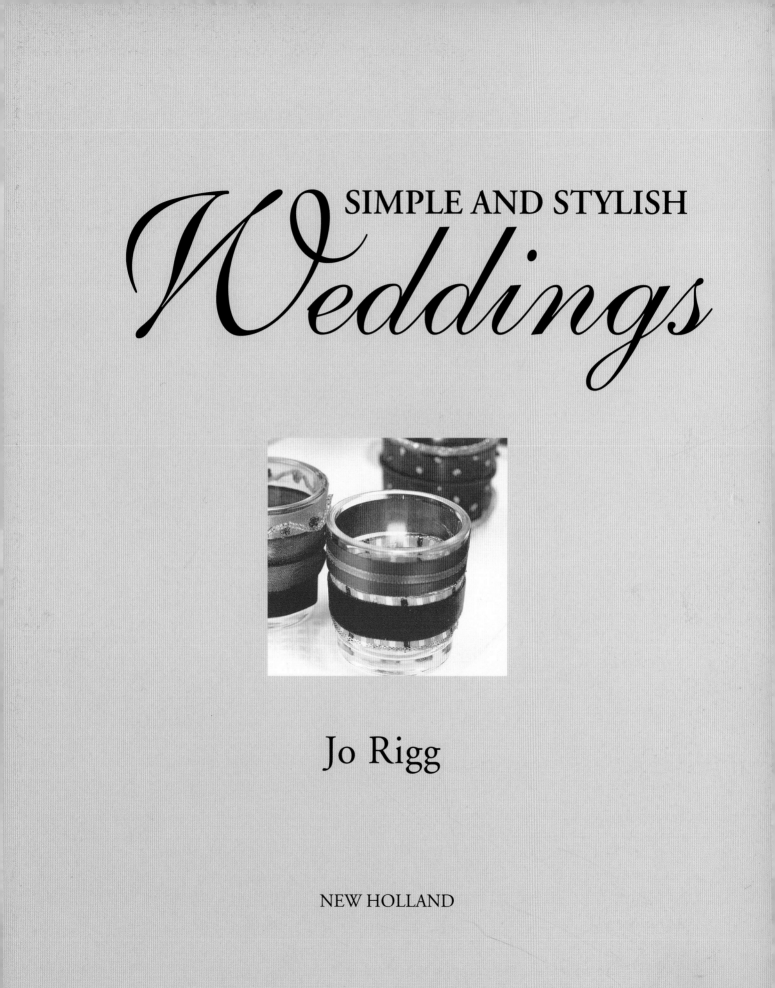

Jo Rigg

NEW HOLLAND

First published in 2004 by
New Holland Publishers (UK) Ltd
London • Cape Town • Sydney • Auckland

Garfield House, 86–88 Edgware Road
London W2 2EA
United Kingdom
www.newhollandpublishers.com

80 McKenzie Street
Cape Town, 8001
South Africa

Level 1, Unit 4, 14 Aquatic Drive
Frenchs Forest, NSW 2086
Australia

218 Lake Road, Northcote
Auckland
New Zealand

10 9 8 7 6 5 4 3 2 1

ISBN 1 84330 626 3

Senior Editor: Clare Sayer
Photographer: Shona Wood
Design: Isobel Gillan
Production: Hazel Kirkman
Editorial Direction: Rosemary Wilkinson

Reproduction by Pica Digital PTE Ltd,
    Singapore
Printed and bound by Times Offset (M)
    Sdn Bhd, Malaysia

Contents

Introduction

A wedding is a great celebration, not only for the couple but also for their family and friends. Such an event involves planning, decision making and spending money, it is, after all, considered by many to be the most important day of your life. Making your wedding a day to remember may, at times, be a little hectic, but above all it should be a pleasant, enjoyable experience. *Simple and Stylish Weddings* is full of creative projects that are easy to make and can't fail to give good results, and will help make those preparations just a bit more fun.

Some of the items that you want to include in your wedding are surprisingly easy to make, and careful attention to detail can really bring the wedding together with originality and style. From a complete set of wedding stationery to a simple appliquéd napkin, in this book you will find inspirational ideas that can be used during the service and the reception, as well as unique gifts for your guests to keep and items to help you remember the day for many years to come.

Making your own invitations, table decorations or bouquets can be a great way to save a little money, but more importantly, these personal touches will make your wedding truly unique to you. None of the projects need be copied exactly, instead you can use the basic idea as a starting point and alter the design to suit you and your wedding. So don't be afraid to change the flowers I have suggested for your favourite blooms or plants that are seasonal to the big day, or to alter the size of a favour box or the colour of a trim. Take inspiration from the following pages and be bold enough to mould them to your own requirements.

PLANNING

Once you have set a budget and booked the ceremony and reception locations, you can think about a possible theme, a way to tie together all the elements of the day. The theme may be connected with the time of year or the location, or you might want a contemporary or country feel surrounding the whole event. With this in mind you can consider colours – perhaps red and gold to warm up a winter wedding, types of flowers – those in season at the time of the wedding are the least expensive and will not look out of place – even the kind of food or drink you want served. To help you make these decisions you could collate a pile of tear sheets, taken from wedding or fashion magazines, of particular colours and styles that take your fancy. There are also wedding fairs you can visit throughout the year and wedding websites that, as well as offering some good ideas and practical advice on planning, also have their own order lines for anything from favours to sparklers. Asking family and friends for advice when making these decisions gives everyone the chance to feel involved with the big day, and the knowledge of people who have already been through it could be invaluable to you. Some good advice is to keep it simple and always consider your budget.

With these major decisions made, make a list of all the things you need to do, from writing the guest list and sending out invitations to organizing buttonholes and the bridal bouquet. Then itemize the list, deciding what you might like to do yourself and what you want to contract out. Once again budget is important here. You want to make your wedding work for you, but don't be tempted by elaborate, over-the-top themes or get carried away ordering expensive items that could take you way over budget. For example, a small wedding favour that seems relatively inexpensive when purchased singly can actually prove to be a very costly decision when given to every guest.

The list then needs to be itemized by timings. What can you do well in advance of the day and what should you leave to the last

minute? Stationery, which should tie into your theme just as much as the flowers, is a good example of something you can be getting on with straight away. You will need to send the invitations out in advance anyway, so why not make a start on the order of service, table numbers and menus at the same time? Placecards and favour boxes will need to be done once the number of guests is confirmed, usually two weeks before the day, likewise the champagne flutes and trimmed napkins, although, of course, you can make a start on these items up to three months before the wedding. The rose petal confetti needs to be made at least four to six weeks in advance and the paper cones can be made ahead of time, all ready to be filled on the day. Fresh flowers can be ordered well in advance, but the

arrangements cannot be created until the last minute. So if you are making your own bouquet, buttonholes, bridesmaid's flowers or a table swag, you will probably be doing so the night before, or even on the morning of, the big day: this is another good time to involve friends and family, who will probably be only too pleased to help out. However, much of the preparation for these projects can be done in advance – for example you could decorate the glass containers with frosting spray for the table centrepieces once the number of tables is confirmed and the organza-draped chairs can be prepared a few days in advance – simply add the floral arrangement at the last minute.

Finally, keep as many notes with your list as you can, because with so much going on it is very easy to forget things. Write down dress-fitting dates, bridemaid's names, addresses and dress sizes and the names of those people you would like to help out with the arrangements, remembering to ask them first and ensure they will be available when you need them. Good planning is essential to the smooth running of your wedding, so keep a notebook and a file of invoices always within easy reach and you will find no difficulty in remaining calm and will be able to enjoy the build up to the big day.

MATERIALS AND EQUIPMENT

Every project features a list of the materials and equipment needed, and many of the items can be used for more than one project. All the materials are readily available in most craft shops or can be purchased mail-order from specialist craft suppliers (see suppliers list on page 79).

Flowers are what most people first think of when considering wedding decorations. Whether you decide to have a florist arrange all or just some of your wedding flowers, it is always a good idea to seek their professional advice. Remember that flowers are seasonal items, and while most flowers are available throughout the year, those that are naturally out of season can be costly. A florist will be able to tell you what is available at a specific time of year and how much particular flowers cost. Show the florist your ideas and they may well have alternative suggestions that would work just as well and not break the budget. Most good florists will be more than happy to make up some of the larger items for your wedding and let you buy the basic materials you need to make up other items yourself, such as the individual blooms, florist's foam (oasis) and florist's wire. A florist will deliver the main arrangements on the day of the wedding, but if you are making your own floral decorations the day before keep the blooms fresh by misting them with water and storing them in a cool dark place.

Ribbons and trims are excellent materials to use for many wedding projects. As well as embellishing floral decorations, they can be used on napkins, favour boxes and even invitations and table centrepieces. They are inexpensive to buy and can be cut to particular lengths.

Handmade papers have a similar quality, they are readily available and have a multitude of uses. Always carefully consider how much you need and try to buy all the paper in one batch, to ensure you get papers that don't vary wildly in colour or pattern, although all handmade papers will vary slightly.

Etch spray and Lazertran paper are more modern craft materials that allow you to transfer a pattern to glass, so you can easily individualize champagne glasses and night-light holders. You will need a photocopying source to use the Lazertran paper. Other specialist craft materials used in the book include metal leaf, which is glued to a surface to give it a metallic finish, and plastic sheet, which is folded to make a fun windmill.

Planning a wedding should be one of the most exciting and magical times and this book will help you turn your wedding day into a really unique occasion. And, above all, it should be fun.

Flowers

Flowers are an essential part of any wedding day — no wedding would be complete without the colour, scent and romance that they provide. Whether it is a bridal bouquet, something smaller for bridesmaids or buttonholes for the groom and his attendants, these stunningly simple floral ideas are easy to make and are guaranteed to make the big day feel extra special.

Bridal bouquet

This floral bouquet is made entirely from gorgeous cream ranunculus. Using one type of flower in this way gives a simplistic and contemporary feel, perfect for a modern wedding. The stems are left long and bound with a length of pink organza ribbon, which is tied quite simply at the front of the bouquet. An arrangement such as this would make a beautiful bridal bouquet or the perfect gift to thank those special friends, family or older bridesmaids who have helped out with the wedding.

1 Gather the flowers together to form a tightly packed bunch and cut all the stems neatly to a length of 30 cm (12 in).

2 While still holding the bunch firmly with one hand, secure the arrangement by wrapping the stems three or four times with florist's wire. Twist the wire tightly closed at the back of the bunch and cut away the excess.

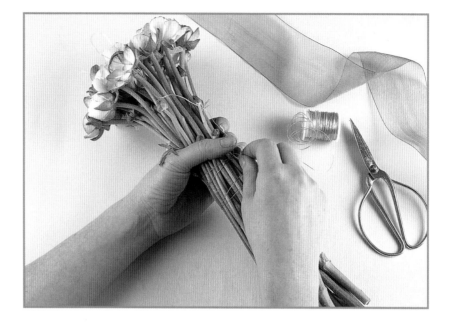

3 Take a 2-m (6½-ft) length of organza ribbon and bind the tightly packed stems several times, making sure you cover the florist's wire as you wrap. Tie the ribbon in the centre of the bouquet with a knot.

♥ *Variation* For a more dramatic look, deep red roses are combined with large green leaves, used at the back of the arrangement to frame the flowers. A length of raffia twine makes an attractive alternative to ribbon.

Buttonholes

YOU WILL NEED

1 large red rose

2 sprigs of rosemary

scissors

green florist's tape

30 cm (12 in) narrow ribbon,
   cord or braid

water mister

*B*uttonholes don't have to be the obligatory plain carnation on a pin, and with these buttonholes there is no need to hide the stems under a lapel because they are attractively covered with tape and ribbon. You can use almost any flower or foliage, but a beautiful red rose makes a simple and elegant buttonhole.

1 Cut the stem of a large red rose and two sprigs of rosemary to a length of 8 cm (3 in). Arrange the rosemary sprigs behind the rose with the stems staggered so that the rosemary sticks out above the flower.

2 Using green florist's tape, begin to bind the stems together. Work from the top downwards, leaving 2.5 cm (1 in) of excess tape at each end to secure the decorative trimming later. Smooth the tape as you work to give a neat finish.

3 Take a 30-cm (12-in) length of narrow ribbon, cord or braid and wind it down the stem, over the top of the green tape. Cut off any excess ribbon.

4 Tuck each end of the ribbon neatly under the florist's tape and press firmly to hold in place. Give the buttonhole a light spray with water to keep the flowers fresh, and store in a cool, dark place until ready to use. Attach the buttonhole to your lapel with a pearl-headed pin pushed gently through the top of the stem.

♥ *Variations* It is possible to fashion a buttonhole from almost any plant. OPPOSITE: *These alternatives feature anenomes (1), freesias tied with ribbon (2), thistle (3) and a variegated carnation (4).*

Floral table swag

YOU WILL NEED

several long lengths of white

winter-flowering jasmine

(enough to run twice the length

or circumference of the table,

plus a few extra lengths

for finishing off)

florist's wire

scissors or wire cutters

tape measure

pencil

drawing pins

white hellebores

water mister

This delicate floral garland has been designed to loop up in between place settings. Winter-flowering jasmine is perfect for a winter wedding, complemented with stunning hellebores. Jasmine also has a wonderful scent, which will fill the air during the wedding meal. The jasmine will last at least a day so the swags can be made the day before.

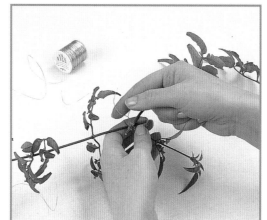

1 Join lengths of jasmine together by first twisting the foliage with your hands, and then securing it at regular intervals with small pieces of florist's wire. Continue until you have a garland that is double the length or circumference of the table.

2 Measure the distance between each place setting and make a light mark at a point halfway between each setting. Attach the jasmine to the table using drawing pins pressed firmly through the foliage and into the table at the marked points.

3 Twist in a few extra lengths of jasmine on top of the table to disguise the drawing pin. The swag can be filled out if necessary in any areas that look a little lighter than others.

4 Slip the stem of an individual hellebore bloom through the foliage on top of the table at each place setting. Trim the hellebore stem when the flower is in its final position, and give the swag a light mist with water to keep it fresh.

Florist's rule *A swag should be twice as long as the length it is to cover. So a table that has a circumference of 4 m (13 ft) should have a swag 8 m (26 ft) in length. Try to balance the 'drop' of the swags so they are even all around.*

Variation

Variegated ivy is always readily available and works extremely well as an alternative to jasmine. Skipping lightly along the table in gentle sweeps, the garland is given a slightly different look with the addition of bows tied from stiff gold ribbon.

Table centrepiece

YOU WILL NEED

- glass container
- self-adhesive shapes
- scrap paper
- protective face mask
- glass etch spray
- wire photograph holder
- white pebbles
- pink hyacinths
- pink roses
- pink tulips
- table number card
- instant photograph or similar
  personal item

A chunky glass, given a coat of frosting spray, provides the base for this modern floral table centre. The arrangement is packed with boldly coloured pink flowers that have intentionally been kept short, making a low arrangement that guests will not have difficulty seeing over.

1 Clean a glass container with hot soapy water to remove any grease or dirt. Stick self-adhesive shapes to the outside of the glass. Turn the glass upside down and place it on a few sheets of scrap paper.

2 In a clean, dry area with good ventilation and wearing a protective face mask, apply an even coat of etch spray to the surface of the glass, following the manufacturer's instructions. When the spray has dried, carefully peel off the self-adhesive shapes.

3 Place a photograph holder centrally inside the container and surround with white pebbles to hold it in place. Add some water, filling the glass half full.

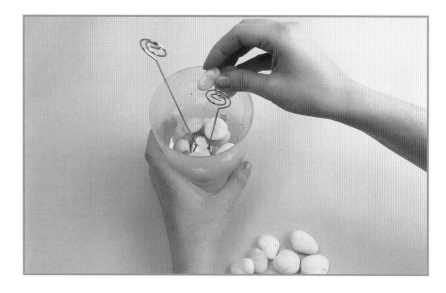

4 Start adding flowers to the container, trimming the stems as you go so the heads are close to the glass rim. The central flowers will need to be a little taller to be seen. The finished arrangement should be slightly domed. Use pebbles to hold the flowers securely in place while you work.

♥ *Variation* *This cost-effective centrepiece uses just three flower heads (gerberas) and a few floating candles in a large glass dish, for an instant and stylish alternative table decoration. An arrangement like this takes minutes to achieve. The candles can be lit as the evening progresses.*

5 Slip a table number card into one arm of the photograph holder and a personal item in the other. Instant photographs are a great addition, taken during and immediately after the wedding service they can be quickly dropped into place just before the guests sit down.

Bridesmaid's flowers

YOU WILL NEED

galvanized metal bucket,

approximately

10 cm (4 in) tall

pliers

small kitchen knife

florist's foam (oasis)

scissors

1 m (40 in) gingham ribbon

1 m (40 in) plain ribbon

hyacinths

*L*ittle galvanized buckets packed full with hyacinths are perfect for small hands to hold and the flowers can be put down and picked up again without being spoiled. A layer of florist's foam soaked in water is hidden inside the bucket to ensure that the flowers stay fresh all day.

1 Remove the metal handles from a galvanized bucket using a pair of pliers. With a small kitchen knife, cut out a round piece of florist's foam (oasis) to fit snugly inside the bottom of the bucket. The foam should be cut to approximately half the height of the bucket.

2 Place the foam inside the bucket and top up with enough water to just cover the foam. The water will quickly be absorbed, ensuring there are no spills or leakage later.

3 Take the two 1-m (40-in) lengths of ribbon and thread both ribbons through the holes at each side of the bucket to form a new handle. Secure the ribbon with a tight knot and trim the ends neatly.

4 Trim the hyacinth stems so that the flower heads are just above the top of the bucket. Cut each stem with a diagonal cut so that they push easily into the florist's foam. Arrange the flowers in the bucket, making sure that there are no gaps and that the arrangement looks good from all angles.

♥ *Variations* *A whole range of everyday items can be transformed into flower carriers to hold most types of flower. Flowerpots, jam jars and even kitchen glasses can all be given this treatment. Tied with ribbon they can be carried by bridesmaids of all ages, although the non-breakable varieties lends themselves more to the younger bridesmaids.*

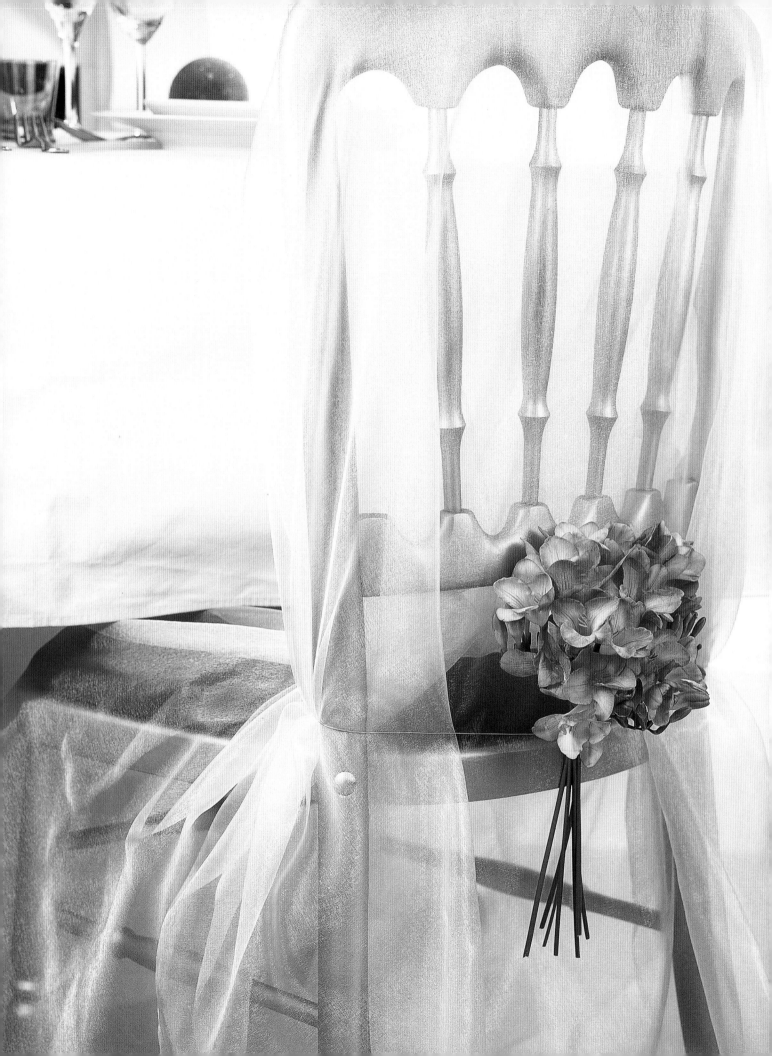

Organza-draped chair

A plain chair dressed with a length of sheer fabric and a bunch of pretty spring flowers adds a romantic look to the celebration. The organza drapes beautifully, catching the light with a sparkle. A simple arrangement of freesias is added at the back of the chair for a simple finish. This project would be a perfect way to decorate the chairs for the top table. The organza can be positioned well in advance, but do not add the flowers until the morning of the wedding.

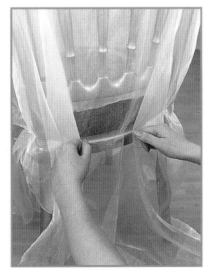

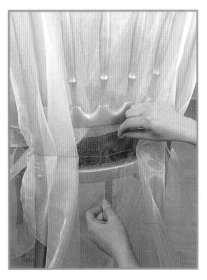

1 Approximately position a 3-m (10-ft) length of sheer fabric over the chair. The fabric should reach the floor at the front of the chair, with a little extra to drape on the floor at the back.

2 Cut a length of florist's wire to fit round the chair back. Roughly find the middle of the wire and position it at the back of the chair seat.

3 Wrap the wire around the chair back and return each end to the central position at the back of the seat. Twist the ends together to secure and cut away any excess wire.

4 Gather together a simple bunch of freesias and trim the stems so they are all the same length.

5 Tie the flowers together with a small length of wire twisted around the stems. Twist the wire on the bunch around the wire at the back of the chair, securing the flowers in place with a little extra wire, if necessary.

♥ *Variation* *Highly colourful silk hydrangeas make a strong statement tied to the back of this chair. Using silk or dried flowers can be the perfect solution when time is short; the chairs can be dressed well ahead of the big day and the flowers require little or no maintenance when finished.*

Table decorations

BEAUTIFUL HANDMADE ITEMS DISPLAYED ON YOUR WEDDING TABLES WILL ADD A STYLISH TOUCH TO THE OCCASION AND WILL CREATE A LASTING IMPRESSION ON YOUR GUESTS, WHETHER YOU ARE PLANNING A FORMAL DINNER OR A MORE CASUAL BUFFET. DECORATED TABLE LINEN, CLEVER IDEAS TO DRESS UP CANDLES AND ELEGANT FLORAL CHAMPAGNE FLUTES ALLOW YOU TO CREATE THE PERFECT SETTING FOR A TRULY UNIQUE OCCASION.

Candle holders

YOU WILL NEED

glass night-light holder

scissors

selection of decorative

  ribbons and trims

glue gun

night-light

*D*ecorated with bands of brightly coloured ribbon, these glass night-light holders are instantly transformed into stylish table decorations. Candlelight has an amazing quality and can turn a celebration into a magical occasion. Beautiful burnt orange colours tie in with an autumn wedding theme, but you could use any colours, and the candle holders will look stunning whether they are scattered randomly about the table or displayed in groups.

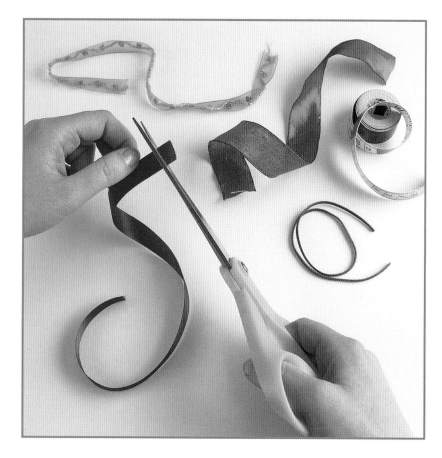

1 Cut several strips of ribbon and trim to wrap around the outside of a glass night-light holder, allowing an extra 1 cm (½ in) to overlap at the back of the holder for a neat finish.

2 Run a line of glue along the reverse of each strip and carefully place it round the glass, pressing firmly in place. The strip should overlap neatly at the back; a little extra glue will help keep it in place. If you are using a ribbon that is more prone to fraying, fold each end under as you work.

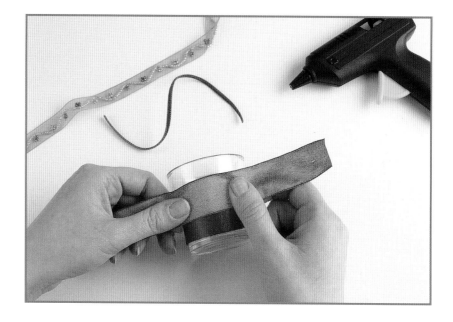

3 Continue adding bands of colour until you have covered the glass. Allow the glue to dry then place a night-light in the glass.

Variation For an alternative idea, skeleton leaves can be wrapped around the outside of the glass holder. The leaves are held in place with a length of fine florist's wire, which has been threaded with a few glass beads before being twisted closed. A coloured night-light finishes the look.

Trimmed napkin

YOU WILL NEED

large white linen napkin

dressmaker's pencil

approximately 3 m
   (10 ft) decorative trim

dressmaker's pins

sewing needle

sewing thread, in a similar
   colour to the trim

scissors

A beautiful trim can really transform a plain white napkin. The trim is hand stitched on in minutes and can be used to subtly introduce a particular colour to the table, perhaps to tie in with a flower arrangement or candle colour. Synonymous with love, the heart is the obvious choice for a wedding motif.

1 Lightly sketch a heart shape on to the right side of a large white napkin using a dressmaker's pencil. The pencil mark will naturally disappear in a few days.

2 Take a 3-m (10-ft) length of decorative trim and pin it directly on to the napkin following the heart-shaped outline as closely as possible.

3 Sew the trim in place by oversewing with small stitches and then remove the pins. Cut the ends of the trim for a neat finish. Pin and sew the remaining trim around the edge of the napkin to complete the look.

Variation In this alternative the napkin decoration has been taken a stage further with a little extra adornment. Find a suitable image such as a cherub and photocopy on to a piece of white paper. Paint over the image with a coat of image transfer paste (see page 79 for stockists) and then place face down in position on to the surface of the napkin. When the paste has dried, simply remove the paper with a damp sponge, leaving the cherub image permanently on the surface of the napkin. Surrounded by a deep red trim the napkin is further decorated with a few sequins for an eye-catching detail.

Gilded table markers

YOU WILL NEED

large flat pebble

soft cloth

scrap paper

size (gilding adhesive)

small paintbrush

silver-coloured metal leaf

soft brush

82 cm (32 in) of 2-mm (14 SWG)
   flexible aluminium wire

round-nosed pliers

card

scissors

A large pebble covered with silver leaf makes an unusual and thoroughly inventive way for guests to identify their table numbers. Metallic leaf is easy to apply and works especially well on the smooth, flat surface of the pebble. A curl of aluminium wire twists around the stone, arching up to form a cardholder, perfect for modern table settings.

1 Wash a large, flat pebble in hot soapy water and dry thoroughly with a soft cloth. Lay the pebble on some scrap paper and paint a layer of size (gilding adhesive) all over it.

2 After approximately 15 minutes, when the size should be slightly tacky but not quite fully dry, you can apply the first sheet of silver-coloured metal leaf. Hold the metal leaf by its backing sheet and place it silver side down on the pebble. Use your fingertips to smooth the leaf down to cover as much of the pebble as possible.

3 Carefully peel off the backing sheet and brush away any loose silver leaf with a clean, dry soft brush. Repeat steps 2–3 until the whole pebble is covered with silver leaf. Add a little more size to any gaps and use the small bits of loose leaf to fill them.

4 Position the pebble on a 82-cm (32-in) length of 2-mm (14 SWG) aluminium wire. Wrap the wire around the base of the pebble and twist it firmly on top to keep in place.

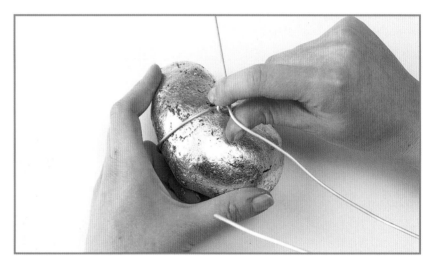

5 Use round-nosed pliers to make a loop at one end of the wire. Hold the loop in the pliers and bend it round to form a coil. Repeat at the other end of the wire. Print or write your table numbers on to card, cut them to size and slide them into the holders ready for use.

Variation A small pebble is roughly covered with gold-coloured metal leaf to make an instant and stylish place card. This time the pebble is lightly stippled with size, allowing small patches of the pebble to remain visible between the gold leaf decoration. Thread the name of the guest on a length of twine and tie it around the pebble. Gilded pebbles could also double as useful weights to keep napkins in place on an outdoor table.

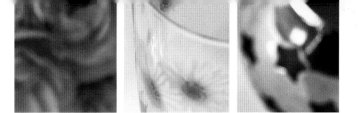

Celebration flutes

YOU WILL NEED

motif, such as chain of flowers
    (see overleaf)

image transfer paper (see
    page 79 for stockists)

champagne flute

small scissors

shallow bowl

paper towel

oven

This pretty daisy design really transforms a set of plain champagne flutes. Using image transfer paper, the motif is easily applied to the outside of a plain glass and after a few minutes in a hot oven you have a permanent reminder of your special day.

1 Make a colour photocopy of your motif directly on to image transfer paper. This daisy design, printed overleaf, fits around the 20-cm (8-in) circumference at the top of a champagne flute, but you can choose any motif. Carefully cut the image out with a pair of small sharp scissors.

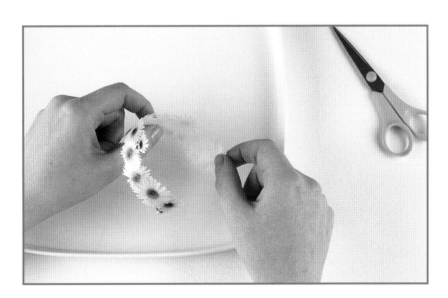

2 Fill a shallow bowl with warm water and lay the cut-out image face down in it. Allow to soak for a few minutes.

3 Remove the image and lay it face down on a sheet of absorbent paper towel, to remove any excess water.

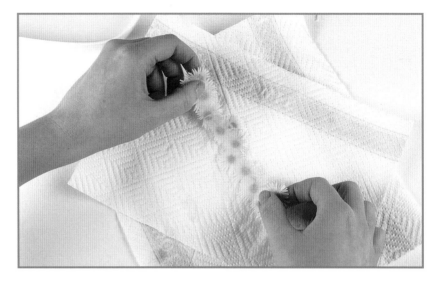

4 Carefully pick up the image and pull a little of the backing paper off. Position the transfer on the surface of the clean, dry glass.

5 Smooth the image with your fingertips as you work round the glass, pulling away the backing paper as you go. Leave to dry overnight. To permanently seal the image, heat the glass gently in the oven, following the manufacturer's guidelines. The transferred image will then harden into enamel.

♥ *Variation* This little dish, decorated with pictures of penny sweets, brings back fond memories of happy childhood days. Filled with a few real sweets for an instant treat, it is sure to be loved by guests of all ages, and makes a pretty favour to take away.

Confetti & favours

*W*HETHER YOU ARE OFFERING YOUR GUESTS
EXQUISITELY WRAPPED FAVOURS OR BEAUTIFUL HANDMADE
PAPER CONES FILLED WITH DELICIOUSLY SCENTED ROSE
PETAL CONFETTI, THESE IMAGINATIVE ITEMS WILL GIVE
YOUR GUESTS SOMETHING SPECIAL TO REMEMBER YOUR
WEDDING DAY BY. THESE PROJECTS ARE NEITHER
EXPENSIVE NOR COMPLICATED TO MAKE AND CAN BE
PREPARED WELL AHEAD OF THE BIG DAY.

Confetti cones

A little forward planning, four to six weeks to preserve the petals, is all that is needed to produce this wonderful confetti, made to a simple recipe. Rich in colour and texture, the confetti also has a beautiful scent. Home-made confetti looks fabulous offered to guests in paper cones. The cones, rolled from a sheet of handmade paper, are tied with a length of ribbon for a little extra decorative finishing detail.

1 Carefully pull apart the flower heads of pale-coloured roses with your fingers. Lay the petals and heads on a cooling rack and place in a warm place to dry for a few hours – a sunny window ledge or an airing cupboard would be ideal.

2 Take a handful of petals and heads and place in a plastic storage box. Add a good sprinkling of salt before adding another layer of petals and heads. Keep building up the layers, finishing with a layer of salt.

3 Press the whole mixture using a flat plate weighted down by a heavy stone. Close the box's lid and leave for four to six weeks.

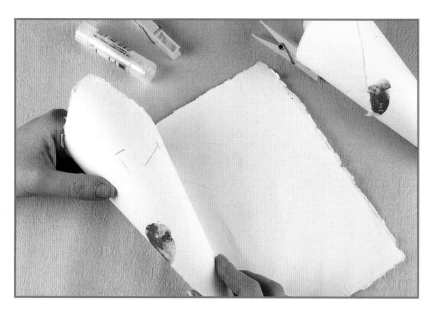

4 To make a cone, lay a sheet of handmade paper flat on a table. Run a line of glue along the right-hand short edge, then roll the sheet from the left-hand short edge into a cone shape. To stop the cone unravelling, hold it in place with a clothes peg until the glue is dry.

Tip Bottle or glass holders are ideal for holding the freshly filled cones of confetti. Alternatively, you could pack them into a large basket and leave it by the entrance to the venue for guests to help themselves.

5 Wrap a 20-cm (8-in) length of ribbon around the cone and tie into a knot to secure. If necessary, you can dab a spot of glue on the cone to keep the ribbon from slipping off. Trim the ribbon ends for a neat finish and fill up with the dried confetti mixture.

Variation The purest white roses mixed with freshly picked lavender makes a stunning alternative confetti mix. The mixture naturally deepened in colour to a gentle yellow as it dried. The roses and lavender were dried separately and mixed together at the last minute, just before dividing into the cones.

Ribboned favour boxes

YOU WILL NEED

thick white card (that will work in

a photocopier)

scissors

metal ruler

cutting mat

craft knife

glue stick

selection of decorative ribbons and trims

*T*hese stunning boxes for wedding favours make a stylish arrangement piled high on a simple china cake stand. They are easily made and in minutes are ready to be filled with a variety of goodies; chocolates or sweets are always a popular choice. For a finishing touch the boxes are decorated with a selection of gorgeous ribbons and trims that can be as elaborate or as colourful as you wish.

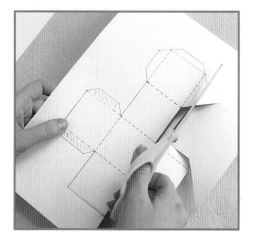

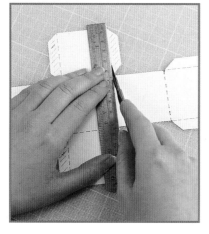

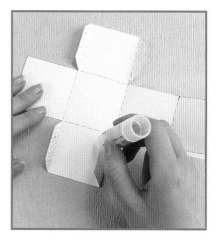

1 Photocopy the template given on page 63 directly on to a sheet of thick white card. Shade in the tabs as on the diagram and cut out the card template.

2 Lay the card on a cutting mat and use a craft knife and metal ruler to lightly score along the dotted lines.

3 Gently fold over each scored line and glue the reverse side of the shaded tabs to close up the body of the box, leaving a lid that can be tucked into the box.

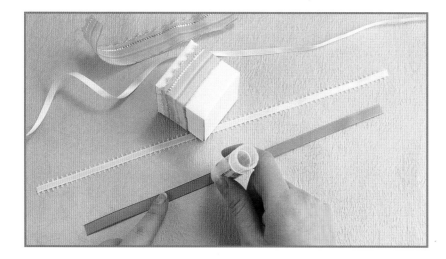

4 To decorate the box, cut 26-cm (10-in) lengths of decorative ribbon and trim. Run a line of glue along the reverse of each strip and press it into place, folding the raw ends under for a neat finish. Overlap different colours and widths of ribbons to achieve the look. Fill the box as you wish.

♥ *Variation* Sugared almonds are traditionally given as favours and these pretty packages would look gorgeous on any table. Clear cellophane bags are filled with sugared almonds and then tied with pretty coordinating ribbon.

Stationery

*M*AKING YOUR OWN WEDDING STATIONERY GIVES

YOU THE CHANCE TO REALLY SET THE MOOD FOR THE

OCCASION. INVITATIONS, ORDER OF SERVICE SHEETS, PLACE

CARDS AND THANK YOU NOTES ARE ALL ITEMS THAT CAN

BE COORDINATED TO SUIT YOUR OWN COLOUR SCHEME.

A MEMORY ALBUM TO STORE ALL THOSE TREASURED ITEMS

IS SIMPLE BUT EFFECTIVE, WHILE SOME COLOURFUL

WINDMILLS ADD A TOUCH OF FUN TO THE CELEBRATIONS.

Handmade invitations

YOU WILL NEED

- thick card (A4 or smaller)
- envelope
- selection of handmade
  papers
- ruler
- scissors
- glue stick
- jeweller's beading wire
- clear tape

Created from an assortment of beautiful layered papers, a home-made invitation is always a pleasure to receive. With an almost limitless choice of textured and coloured papers available, and a design that could be altered to suit, it is possible to create your own original theme, that could also be extended to order of service cards, menus and place cards.

1 Fold a sheet of thick card in half to make the main part of the invitation, making sure that it will fit your envelope.

2 Make a series of rectangles of varying sizes from the textured card and handmade papers selected. The handmade papers can be given a soft-feathered finish by folding the edges firmly then tearing gently down the fold against the side of a ruler. Thicker edges of a piece of card are best cut with scissors.

3 Layer the rectangles on top of each other until you are happy with the arrangement. Glue the rectangles together then stick the whole arrangement in place on the front of the main card.

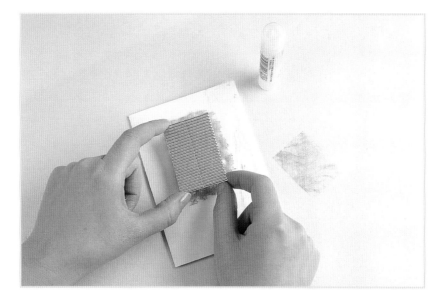

4 Use your fingers to form a heart shape from a length of jeweller's beading wire. Twist the ends of the wire tightly together and pierce them through the front of the card. Tape the ends of the wire securely on the inside.

♥ *Variation* *Place cards are made in the same way, just on a smaller scale. Other items can also be adapted to fit the scheme; for example, menus or other printed items can be printed first and have the decoration added later. Here, the blue works well with cool silver, but a red and gold theme would be equally stunning.*

Memory album

ruler

fine marker pen

sheet of A4-sized tin plate

scissors

blunt pencil

glue gun

photograph or

keepsake album

*C*ollect and store some wonderful wedding keepsakes and precious mementos in this beautiful memory album. In this personalized album you can store photographs and cards, and perhaps the order of service and menu. Made from readily available and inexpensive materials, the album decoration can be adapted to suit any couple and will add a really special touch to your collection of favourite memories.

1 Using a ruler and marker pen, measure and mark a rectangle 7 × 9 cm (2¾ × 3½ in) directly on to a tin plate sheet. Cut out carefully with scissors.

2 Using the design on page 73 as a guide, copy the motif on to the tin rectangle with the marker pen. Don't worry if your design is not exactly the same as the one in the photograph – the pattern is just meant as a guide. If you make a mistake, you can wipe the tin plate clean with a soft cloth.

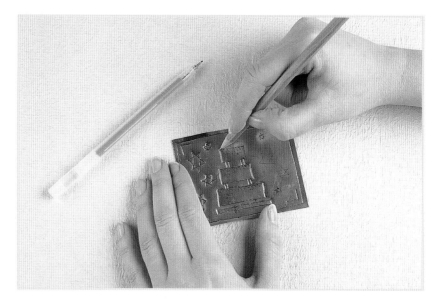

3 Using a blunt pencil, trace over the marker pen lines, using a firm but even pressure.

4 Turn the embossed panel over and apply several spots of glue to the reverse. Position the panel on the album and leave to dry.

♥ *Variation As well as photographs and cards, you will find there are all sorts of other items you want to keep as mementoes. This keepsake box is perfect for storing things like confetti, champagne corks or a dried flower from the bouquet. The technique is the same as for the memory album – simply create your own design or use the heart motif on page 73.*

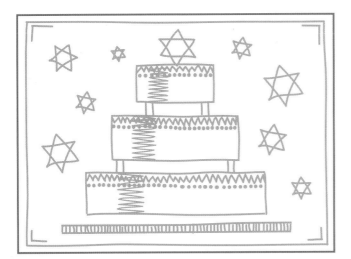

Design for memory album

Design for keepsake box

Decorative windmills

YOU WILL NEED

A4 sheet of polypropylene
plastic (available from
good craft suppliers)

permanent marker pen

ruler

strong scissors

hole punch

map pin

30 cm x 8 mm (12 x ¼ in)
wooden dowelling

These eye-catching windmills add a colourful touch of fun to a modern table. Guaranteed to be popular with younger guests, the windmills could be grouped together on each table or pushed into the ground on each side of a pathway, leading the guests into the party.

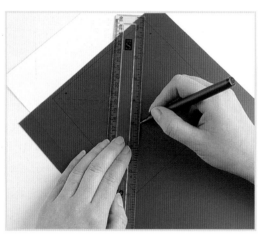

1 Photocopy the windmill template on page 78. Lay the photocopy face up on a table and place a sheet of polypropylene on top. Using a marker pen and ruler, trace the pattern directly on to the plastic sheet. Where the template indicates small circles, mark these freehand.

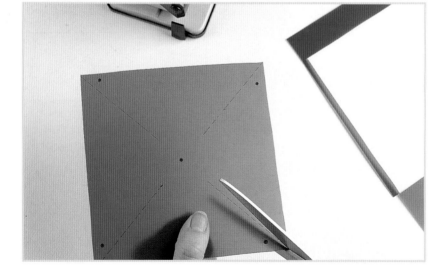

2 Cut the pattern out with a pair of strong scissors, then cut along the diagonal lines. Use a hole punch to carefully punch through the single circles at each corner.

3 Fold over each punched corner and bring it into the middle of the windmill, working in a clockwise pattern. Carefully thread a map pin through the four punched holes. Push the point of the pin through to the back of the windmill, piercing the plastic behind through the central circle marked on the template.

4 Holding the windmill tightly with your fingers, push the map pin and windmill firmly into a piece of wooden dowelling 30 cm x 8 mm (12 x ¼ in) until secure.

♥ *Variation A small yellow windmill makes a delightfully quirky decoration for a celebration dessert – this one is secured with a drawing pin. The miniature scale is kept in perfect proportion by reducing the template down with a photocopier.*

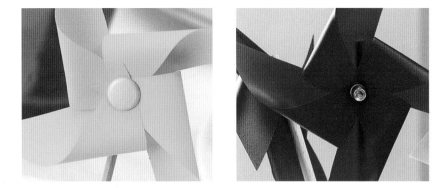

Template for windmill

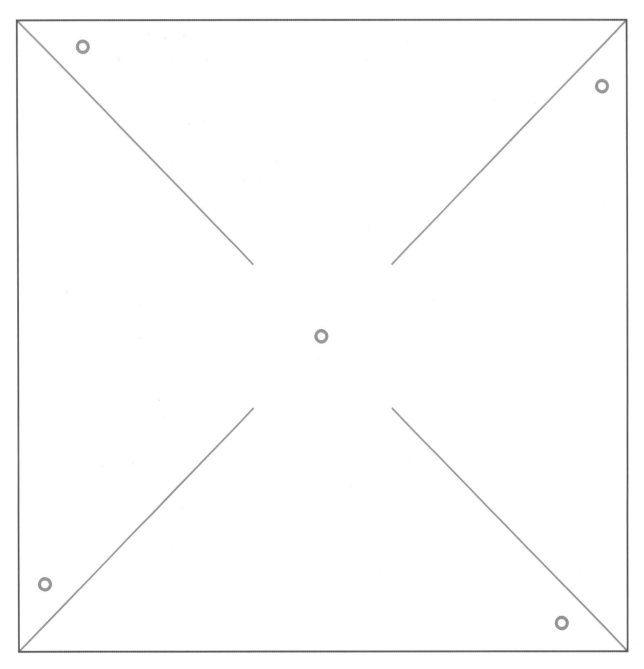

SUPPLIERS AND USEFUL
ADDRESSES

UK

Confetti
80 Tottenham Court Road
London W1T 4TF
Tel: (020) 7436 7177
www.confetti.co.uk
Wedding/party shop and website.

The Dover Bookshop
18 Earlham Street
London WC2H 9LG
Tel: (020) 7836 2111
www.doverbooks.co.uk
Suppliers of copyright-free images.
Mail order available.

Dylon International Ltd
Worsley Bridge Road
Lower Sydenham
London SE26 5HD
Tel: (020) 8663 4801
www.dylon.co.uk
Suppliers of image transfer paste (see
page 45). Mail order service available.

Jongor Events Catering Equipment
& Furniture Hire
Tel: (020) 8443 3333
Fax: (020) 8443 6192
For silver chairs (see page 32).
Branches throughout the UK.

Lazertran Ltd
8 Alban Square, Aberaeron
Dyfed SA46 0AD
Tel: (01545) 571149
www.lazertran.com
Suppliers of image transfer and wet
release paper (see page 51).

Paperchase
213 Tottenham Court Road
London W1P 9AF
Tel: (020) 7580 8496
www.paperchase.co.uk
Large selection of papers, cards, pens,
photograph albums and other
stationery items. Mail order available.

Specialist Crafts Ltd
PO Box 247
Leicester LE1 9QS
Tel: (0116) 269 7733
www.homecrafts.co.uk
Large selection of art materials and
craft supplies. Mail order available.

AUSTRALIA

Artwise Amazing Paper
186 Enmore road
Enmore, NSW 2042
Tel: (02) 9519 8237

Greta's Handcraft Centre
321 Pacific Highway
Lindfield, NSW 2070
Tel: (02) 9416 2489

Heidelburg Fine Arts
44–46 Greeves Street
Fitzroy, Victoria 3065
Tel/fax: (03) 9419 4232
Email: neil@hfaw.com.au

Lincraft
www.lincraft.com.au
General craft supplier. Stores
throughout Australia

NEW ZEALAND

Gordon Harris Art Supplies
4 Gillies Ave, Newmarket
Auckland
Tel: (09) 520 4466
Fax: (09) 520 0880

www.weddingaccessories.net.nz

SOUTH AFRICA

Arts, Crafts and Hobbies
12 Hibernia Street
George 6529
Tel/fax: (044) 874 1337

The Crafter's Den
17 2nd Avenue
Orange Grove 2192
Johannesburg
Tel: (011) 483 0563

INDEX

1 DOMANI

1 DOMANI